The Fort

CW01023979

By Alison Hawes
Illustrations by Jon Stuart

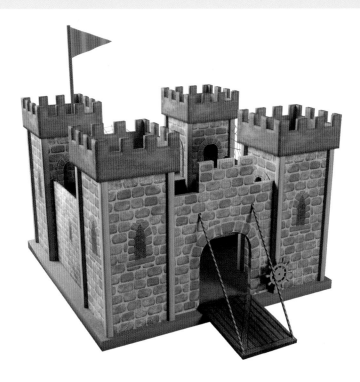

OXFORD
UNIVERSITY PRESS

In this story ...

- Introduce children to the characters in this story: Cat, Tiger and Tiger's dad.
- Point to the words that represent the characters' names and say each of the names together. Children will meet these words in the story.

Cat

Tiger

Tiger's dad

📖 READ

Cat and Tiger have special watches. When they push the buttons on their watches they can shrink to micro-size, like this …

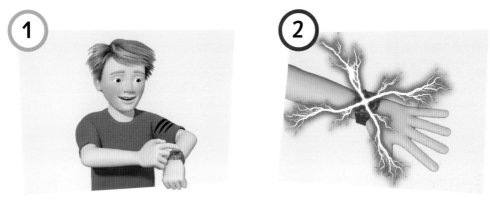

They become tiny and can have amazing adventures!

📖 READ

One day, Tiger's dad found a box of his old toys in the attic. They were covered in dust and cobwebs but, otherwise, they were as good as new.

"This was my favourite when I was little," smiled Dad, picking up the fort. "I think I'll give it to Tiger."

💬 TALK

- Tell children what an attic is. Talk about what might be stored in an attic.

👥 ACTIVITY

- Point to the word *light* on the page and ask children to count how many letters there are in the word.
- Then ask children to sound-talk the word *light* (i.e. light becomes l-igh-t).
- Repeat the activity with the words *boat*, *train* and *car*.

✦ Tip

See the inside back cover for more guidance on sounds.

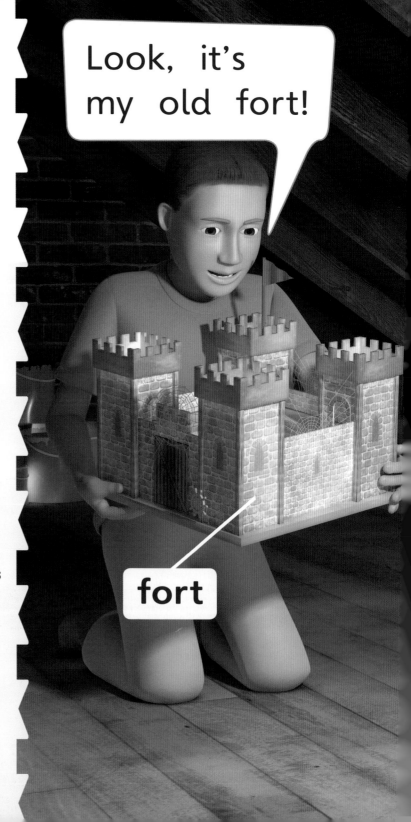

Look, it's my old fort!

fort

light

train

boat

car

book

📖 READ

Later that day, Cat came round to see Tiger. He showed her the fort that his dad had given him. "Ooh cool!" said Cat. "Imagine *living* in a fort!"

"Let's shrink and then we can pretend we live in this one!" said Tiger excitedly.

"Great idea!" laughed Cat.

💬 TALK

- Talk about the fort and ask children if they can think of other words that are used for buildings that look like this (e.g. castle, fortress).

👥 ACTIVITY

- Point to the word *cool* on the page and ask children to sound-talk it (i.e. cool becomes c-oo-l).
- Then ask children to blend the sounds together and say the word (i.e. c-oo-l becomes cool).
- Repeat the activity with the word *fort*.

This fort was my dad's.

📖 READ

Cat and Tiger pushed the buttons on their watches to shrink to micro-size.

Cat couldn't wait to get inside. She ran straight up on to the ramparts.

"Wait for me!" shouted Tiger, hurrying towards the drawbridge.

💬 TALK

- Point out some of the features of a fort and their purpose:
  - **Drawbridge** The purpose of a drawbridge was to allow or prevent entry to the fort.
  - **Thin windows** Thin windows were used for shooting arrows at the enemy. Thin windows meant arrows were less likely to get into the fort.
- **Have some fun!** Ask children to design and make their own fort using cardboard boxes, string, straws, paper, etc.

Wait for me!

📖 READ

Cat tried to hurry Tiger along. "Come on, Tiger! It's great up here!"

Tiger wasn't so sure. The fort was dark and full of cobwebs. Tiger knew that where there were cobwebs, there were spiders … He did not like spiders!

💬 TALK

• Talk about how Tiger is feeling.

👥 ACTIVITY

• Say the following sentence: *Insects might get stuck in a web.* Ask children to sound-talk the word *might* (i.e. might becomes m-igh-t).

• Ask children to write the word *might*. How many letters are there in the word? Children could use magnetic letters, a whiteboard or a pencil and paper to write.

• If children find this easy, they could try to write the whole sentence.

It is too dark. I need a light.

Tiger thought he saw something lurking in the shadows. He flicked on the light on his watch ... Something moved.

Tiger let out a yelp. It was a spider! Tiger turned pale with terror but he couldn't move.

💬 TALK

- Tell children some spider facts:
  - Spiders have eight legs.
  - They have either six or eight eyes.
  - Spider silk is very strong.
  - Not all spiders spin webs.
  - Most spiders are harmless.
- **Have some fun!** Ask children to design their own spiders and webs using wool, crepe paper, egg boxes, glitter, etc.

Cat and Tiger ran from the fort.

📖 READ

Tiger was too frightened to move.

Cat shook him gently. "Come on," she whispered. "Let's get out of here!"

Tiger turned and sprinted for the doorway. Cat could barely keep up with him.

💬 TALK

- Ask children to think of words to describe how Cat and Tiger are feeling. Use this as an opportunity to extend their vocabulary (e.g. petrified, terrified).

👥 ACTIVITY

- Read out the following sentence: *Quick, step on the carpet*. Ask children to sound-talk the word *quick* (i.e. quick becomes qu-i-ck).
- Then ask children to blend the sounds together and say the word (i.e. qu-i-ck becomes quick).
- Ask children to write the word *quick*. How many letters are there in the word?

The spider scuttled after them but they escaped just in time. Cat and Tiger turned the handle and closed the fort door, trapping the spider inside the fort.

"Time to push the buttons!" gasped Tiger. It was not always fun being micro-size!

- Point to the word *keep* on the page and ask children to sound-talk it (i.e. keep becomes k-ee-p).
- Then ask children to blend the sounds together and say the word (i.e. k-ee-p becomes keep).

My dad can keep his fort!

Quick, Tiger! Help me turn this!